FEAR and HOPE:

Toward Political Democracy in Central America

by Penny Lernoux

The Field Foundation
100 East 85th Street
New York, NY 10028

571

CENTRAL AMERICA

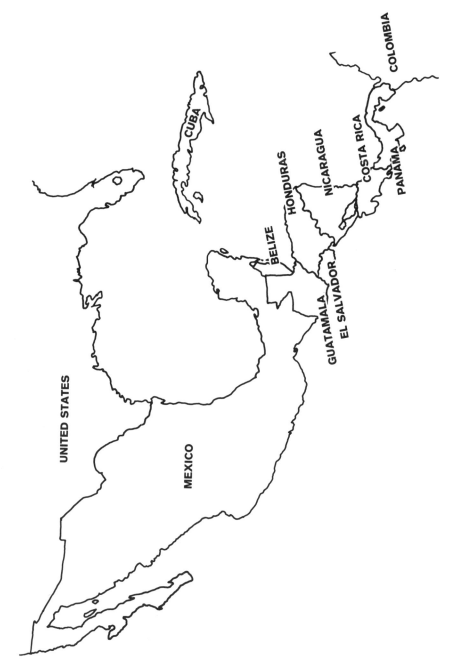

UNITED STATES

MEXICO

CUBA

BELIZE

GUATAMALA

EL SALVADOR

HONDURAS

NICARAGUA

COSTA RICA

PANAMA

COLOMBIA

Contents

	Page
INTRODUCTION: The Cultural Context	6
PART I: Peace–the Precondition for Democratic Growth in Central America	14
PART II: Democratic Growth–Organizations and Methods	25
PART III: An Action Plan	34

FOREWORD

Since its beginning in 1940, the Field Foundation has been concerned with easing the burden of poverty and racial injustice and protecting those civil liberties so basic to a free society. Over the years, it has become increasingly evident that issues of social justice, civil rights and civil liberties are nation-wide, complex and often related to international events. Escalation of the arms race, global inflation, deprivation of human rights and large and small wars around the world affect the lives of all Americans but have a particularly adverse effect upon the lives of children and families attempting to cope day by day with ordinary stress.

While the Foundation's work has been largely focused on domestic problems, periodically it has undertaken efforts extending beyond the nation's borders. Precedent can be found in the personal and practical assistance Marshall Field III gave to children of Great Britain during World War II when he brought many to the United States for safekeeping and education. Through the years, the Foundation has been enriched by the insight and recommendations of such trustees active in international and foreign affairs as the late Adlai Stevenson and Ralph Bunche, of the United Nations, and Clarence Pickett, Nobel Prize winner, with the American Friends Service Committee. For the Foundation to remain faithful to its humanitarian responsibilities, the trustees considered it proper, indeed imperative, that it pay attention to the state of affairs in other countries when political policies and practices seemed to abuse the well-being of children and families and our sense of decency and justice.

So in addition to attacking the domestic problems of racism, poverty and threats to civil liberties, Field has supported efforts to combat racial tyranny in South Africa and Southwest Africa and provided aid to the "boat people" of Indochina. In both domestic and international concerns, the Foundation has sought to initiate programs and to find partnerships and allies in order to encourage common efforts to effect changes to better the lot of the disadvantaged.

It is natural then for the Field Foundation to note with extreme concern what is happening to children and families in Central America. In this region are found some of the world's most repugnant examples of oppression ranging from the denial of basic needs to torture and execution. From such concern came a decision to seek expert assistance in assessing the state of affairs in that part of this hemisphere, a region in which our country has great inter-

4

est and a large measure of responsibility, and about which Americans are confused by reports that are often contradictory and purposefully misleading.

Accordingly, the Foundation obtained the help of Penny Lernoux, a person with first-hand knowledge of the culture, history, and political and economic affairs of Latin America, where she has lived for twenty-three years. She is also a journalist of distinction, the recipient of the Tom Wallace Award from the Inter-American Press Association and the press award from the Latin American Studies Association. For her book, *Cry of the People,* Ms. Lernoux received both the Sidney Hillman Foundation Book Award and Columbia University's Maria Moors Cabot Award.

We believe that her carefully researched and scholarly analysis has special value because of her sensitivity to the views of Latin Americans. Her recommendations for helping them achieve political democracy represent a practical and realistic alternative to proposals from groups whose studies so often are short-ranged, biased and fragmented, and based on anecdotal material collected in episodic visits by persons unfamiliar with the history, the culture or even the language of the people there.

The Field Foundation's interest in Central America and in other foreign countries does not signal a lessening of interest in domestic issues, but a complement to it. As Americans, we are aware that money spent on wars, their preparation and their residue deprives our needy citizens of funds basic to their livelihood and well-being; in the case of children, of adequate food, better shelter, high quality education and medical care. This deprivation is accompanied by an emotional, ethical and moral heritage of war: fear, guilt, racial hatred and insensitivity to human life and human values. The Field Foundation believes that American strength in the world must rely more on our commitment to freedom, social and economic justice and to understanding and acceptance of cultural differences at home and abroad than on hostility and strife amongst ourselves or our neighbors.

In that spirit, we present this paper to all who feel a responsibility to the children now living and to those who will follow, whether they be our own or those of our neighbors.

Milton J.E. Senn, Vice-President, Field Foundation
Southbury, CT
February 13, 1984

INTRODUCTION

Many recent papers and articles describe the problems in Central America and call for a change in U.S. policy toward the region.[1] They cite a long history of suffering by the Central American masses as well as frequent errors by U.S. administrations. The aim here is not to repeat what has been amply stated but to provide a cultural framework for actions that can be taken to foster democratic growth in Central America. Such actions can also serve as a conscious act of protest against current U.S. policy.

Different Ways of Seeing Things

The reason for a cultural emphasis is that what seems paramount to Americans often is of secondary interest to Latin Americans and unworkable in their cultures. An example is freedom of the press. In Latin America, the relative importance of an unshackled press can only be understood in the large context of widespread illiteracy and lack of access to education, often a deliberate government policy.[2] While a sign of political liberalization, the absence of newspaper censorship is less critical than government control of radio stations since the uneducated masses depend on radio for most of their news. In almost every country in Latin America, *including elected democracies*, the government controls and censors the radio networks.

The paper's emphasis on a cultural framework also reflects the writer's 23 years of living in, and reporting on, Latin America. During that time, U.S. governments have experimented with innumerable economic and military aid programs, the best known of which was the Alliance for Progress. Each new program was said to be the definitive solution to Latin America's problems. Yet if success is measured by democratic development, a better standard of living for the majority, and/or more mature relations with the United States, all were failures. Indeed, the last successful diplomatic initiative dates to Roosevelt's Good Neighbor Policy of the 1930's.

When asked why so many tensions exist in U.S.-Latin American relations, local leaders reply that: (1) Washington "doesn't understand us," and (2) the United States lacks any consistent Latin American policy. The second statement underscores the first. Since World War II, U.S. policy has stumbled from one crisis to another instead of providing leadership to avert or at least diminish problems. Thus we react —often with too little too late— instead of taking the initiative with new ideas. For example, had the Carter administration actively supported the reformist junta that came to power in El Salvador in 1979, the course of events might have been different. But Washington was so preoccupied with the crisis in Iran that it paid little attention to developments in El Salvador. When the reformists on the junta most needed U.S. moral support, nobody in Washington was listening. It was not until El Salvador became a crisis, that it was finally understood that the chances for political peace might have died with the junta. But by then it was too late to put the pieces together again.[3]

Washington's failure to heed the Latin Americans–or to see *their* reality through *their* eyes–is a bipartisan failure by Democrats as well as Republicans. The reason is not lack of goodwill but, cultural and political constraints. As Irving Stone once wrote, we are like people "watching a dance from outside through heavy plate glass windows." Though we may report the mechanical gestures with pedantic fidelity, "what rarely comes through ...are the injured racial feelings, the misery, the rankling slights. So (we) do not really understand what leads men to abandon wife, children, home, career, friends, to take to the bush and live gun in hand like a hunted animal; to challenge overwhelming military odds rather than acquiesce any longer in humiliation, injustice, or poverty..."[4]

Stone was writing about Vietnam, but his observation equally applies to the current situation in Central America. As noted by a perceptive American journalist who lived through the Vietnam war, the most striking parallel is the United States' utter failure to understand the complex internal dynamics at work in Third World societies. To force these societies into an American mold, in which the first and often only consideration is a Soviet threat, is to misunderstand completely the historical causes of insurrection.[5]

Fear of Diversity

To hear the music of time, the first requisite is an understanding–not fear–of cultural diversity. Latin Americans have their own, quite different, history and cultural tradition, and they have their own way of seeing and doing things. They do not want to be Americans any more than they want to be Europeans. The tragedy is that the elites' political and economic dependence on Spain and, later, Great Britain and the United States, has prevented all of the Latin American countries from developing an indigenous political system based on their own grassroots traditions of democracy. Thus the half-finished copies of liberalism, capitalism, and communism, all with major flaws, that we find in the region.

Grassroot vs. Military

Concerned Central Americans have rightly pointed out that for political parties–and elections– to have any democratic meaning, they must have the underpinnings of intermediate groups like trade unions, peasant federations, and church communities, or the local equivalent of the early town meetings in New England. Many of these groups have historical traditions of democracy in their internal development, however they may have been repressed by outside forces. It is here, at the community level, that Americans should be listening and where they should be supporting new leaders who are more democratic and responsive to the majority of the people. These grassroots efforts do not need billions of dollars in aid. Huge inflows of money actually distort and smother local endeavors. And those endeavors cannot grow at all if the United States is encouraging a military buildup with enormous outlays on equipment and training, and thus weakening already fragile civilian institutions.

A case in point is Honduras, where U.S. support of the military has been paralleled by the military's crackdown on students and labor unions.[6]

Accustomed to a society in which the armed forces are controlled by civilian institutions, Americans do not always understand that the military in Latin America is often the only political party. It controls the government, the pursestrings, and the right of veto over the judicial system–not to protect national security but to enrich its members and ensure their domination of the civilian population. Those who object to this repressive and corrupt system, including some conservative businessmen, are tarred as "communist," an all-purpose epithet having nothing to do with Marxism. Thus U.S. military aid perpetuates an anti-democratic political system in which the indigenous military serves as an occupying army, and the people are treated as the enemy.

Brief Historical Overview

Of the seven Central American countries, only two do not have a history of internal military occupation–Costa Rica, for ethnic reasons, and Belize, until recently a British colony. Although it has its share of rural inequities, Panama generally follows an independent course on regional matters and, because of the Canal and a banking haven, has a somewhat different economic structure. The "crisis" area is therefore reduced to four countries–El Salvador, Nicaragua, Guatemala, and Honduras, with a combined population of 19.2 million and an annual per capita income of $912. Honduras is the poorest of the four (only Haiti, of all the Latin American nations, is more desperate); El Salvador the most overpopulated. Behind the statistics lies a long history of exploitation of the impoverished masses by a small, wealthy elite (on average two percent of the population) which, in partnership with the military, has controlled most of the agriculture, industry, and trade. Malnutrition and infant mortality are widespread, and repeated messages have conditioned many of the people to think of themselves as little more than slaves. The 1932 bloodbath in El Salvador, in which an estimated 30,000 peasants were killed, and genocidal attacks by the Guatemalan military on the country's helpless Indians are but two examples. The other common denominator is repeated U.S. military intervention—at least two dozen since the turn of the century.[7] In the region's semi-feudal societies, insurrections are bound to occur—and have occurred repeatedly since the end of the 19th century. Eventually, and inevitably, they are successful, as in Nicaragua, where the Somoza dynasty was overthrown in 1979 after 43 years of struggle.

South America is different, and the difference is revealing. Though the region's countries have suffered long periods of military dictatorship, they have also known democratically elected governments. Because there is hope for an alternative, guerrilla movements have not succeeded. In the crisis countries of Central America, on the other hand, all avenues to change have been closed, not just for a few years but for centuries. (The one attempt at change through reform, rather than revolution, was destroyed in Guatemala in 1954, with the help of the CIA.[8]) With no possibility of peaceful change, even the most conservative institutions will support insurrection. In Nicaragua, for example, the country's Catholic bishops justified the Sandinista revolt on the basis of an early church doctrine supporting "just wars against tyrants."*

Two Conditions

In such a context, local efforts to establish democratic institutions need understanding and support, particularly since they go against the weight of history. But understanding is only possible if two conditions exist:

1. Enough facts (versus political or cultural misconceptions) must be available to judge a nuanced situation, both from the U.S. viewpoint and that of the Central Americans, the latter including a broad spectrum of society, not just the defense minister or the head of the local chamber of commerce. Knowledge in turn counsels patience. As shown in other Latin American societies, it takes at least one generation, and perhaps more, to consolidate change, and even longer under agrarian conditions.[9]

2. Grassroots movements must be allowed to develop on their own, even if in the longer term they lead to the emergence of political and

*Even the Kissinger Commision on Central America condeded that local conditions of poverty and injustice lead to rebellions.

economic systems different from our own. Form is less important than content, for there are many different paths to a democratic society.

Nationalism

The United States' fear of diversity –and often hostile response to it– reflects a misunderstanding of nationalism, the historical bearer of change in Latin America and elsewhere in the Third World. Because these nations do not want to be client states of Washington does not automatically mean that they are the United States' enemies. Unfortunately, most U.S. governments since World War II have failed to understand that mature, respectful neighbors offer a more lasting relationship than weak sycophants.

The failure to see that nationalism is more important than ideology has blinded Washington to the nuances of insurrectionist movements. Many Central American guerrilla leaders are Marxists, but that does not mean that they were all educated and trained by foreign communist powers. Despite attempts to label them as Maoist, Castroite, Trotskyite or Soviet, most learned their Marxism at home from firsthand observation of the reality of poverty and repression. As pointed out by many non-Marxists in Central America, including officials of the Catholic Church, Marxism's primary appeal is that it appears to reflect the Central Americans' reality of colonialism and capitalism. By colonialism, they mean the region's traditional political and economic dependence on the United States. *Foreign Affairs* editor William P. Bundy points out that in Central America "we have to deal with the legacy of our own past colonialism— as the area sees it. Key regional countries and the younger generation throughout Latin America see the struggle as primarily due, not just to desperate social and economic conditions, but to Washington's past armed interventions and support for right-wing decadent dictatorships."[10] As to capitalism, the Central American version has much more in common with the primitive model of early 19th century England than the sophisticated, complex forms now practiced in Europe or the United States. When seen in such terms, Marx's appeal to nationalism may be more comprehensible. But what is not always understood is that Marxism is subordinate to nationalism, just as it was in Vietnam.[11]

A nationalistic nation itself, the United States makes a major error in not recognizing the same feelings in others. Instead of rebuffing or denigrating them, it needs to build on common sentiments of nationhood which will outlast ideologies.

Two other interrelated factors need explanation:

Class Divisions

The first is a question of class. Unlike the United States, where class divisions are submerged, Central American attitudes are conditioned by social and racial discrimination. In most of these societies personal achievement counts less than surname, and without the proper surname—and sufficient degree of whiteness—the opportunity for learning and economic advancement is normally denied. In a society in which a small elite controls most of the agricultural and industrial wealth as well as political power,[12] and in which the majority of the people are impoverished and disenfranchised, insurrection is bound to take on the color of class warfare. This was less obvious in Nicaragua, where almost everybody, including the upper classes, supported the effort to oust Somoza. But it is eminently clear in Guatemala, where the downtrodden Indian serfs have begun to join the guerrilla forces.

The inevitability of class influences on the direction of revolution is not always understood in the United States because our cultural framework is so different. Yet if the Nicaraguan elites—or Washington—had stopped to think about the process of revolution, they would have seen immediately that post-war Nicaragua was bound to be a different, less unequal society. The grassroots momentum behind the Sandinistas wanted structural changes, not a country of Somocismo without Somoza, as the elites had intended. And in that respect the Sandinistas have lived up to their revolutionary promise by undertaking a genuine redistribution of wealth. The Salvadoran elites understand the challenge quite well, which is why they have fought change with so much ferocity. Archbishop Oscar Romero, the gentle, martyred archbishop of San Salvador, once warned Salvador's elites to take off their rings before others cut off their fingers. But in societies with sharp class divisions such vision is interpreted as class betrayal, and those of the elite who urge change are killed by their own, as has happened frequently in El Salvador and Guatemala.

Human Rights

Americans' failure to understand the importance of class divisions in the impetus for change is a reflection of the second cultural factor that sets U.S. society apart from that of Latin America—the definition of human rights. In liberal societies like the United States, such rights are normally identified as individual ones—the right to own property, for instance, or freedom of expression. But in the extremely unequal societies of the Third World, such rights are meaningless unless they include the broader ones—the right to live, to eat, to work, to read and write. Such social and economic rights are taken for granted in the United States, but in the semi-feudal societies of Central America the right to survive–which is what the mass of the people are struggling for– must be juxtapositioned alongside the right of a few wealthy people to maintain their individual propertied rights. Unfortunately, this struggle is often portrayed as a few holdouts defending the fortress of free enterprise against marauding Marxists (i.e., Nicaragua), when in reality the issue is much more complex. The ideal is to balance collective and individual rights, and therein lies the importance of the democratic growth of community organizations. But to suggest that "enterprise" has ever been free of class privilege in Central America is to ignore the reality of history.

Historical Importance of Moral Weapons

Economic and political power enables the United States to serve as advocate, not adversary, of change, and thus to influence the tides of history. But the strongest weapon in its arsenal is a moral one: by living up to its historical principles in support of democratic initiatives, the United States can contribute more to good relations with Central America than any amount of money can achieve. Or as a Central American educator put it, "We only want for ourselves what you want for yourselves. If you don't want dictators in the United States, do not support them in our countries."

Political skeptics may scoff at such idealism, but history proves that moral persuasion can be a powerful political tool, as shown by the early Christian communities that challenged and overcame the Roman empire, and by the United States' own beginnings as a nation. In an earlier era the United States was one of the most admired nations among Latin Americans because it stood for the same revolutionary principles that inspired the region's liberators, especially Simón Bolívar. The moral support given Bolívar's cause by the young American republic left a lasting impression that even later decades of intervention and distrust have not completely obliterated. In contrast, the Soviet Union has no such history on which to build relations with its neighbors. (Significantly, Latin Americans say they like Americans even while they dislike their government's policies. This includes the Nicaraguans, who have made a clear distinction between the Reagan administration's hostile policies and the American people, to the point of officially welcoming hundreds of American visitors; giving them free access to all parts of the country, save for military installations; and waiving the requirement of a visa for U.S. citizens.[13])

The Soviet Union has proved an aggressive military occupier of its neighbors; so, too, the United

12

States in Central America and the Caribbean. But there have also been periods in U.S.-Latin American relations, The Good Neighbor policy era, for example, when diplomacy—or a return to principles—was thought to achieve more than militarism. Thus when Mexico expropriated U.S. oil companies in the late 1930s, Roosevelt refused to heed the calls for military intervention. The warmongers predicted dire consequences for U.S. investments elsewhere if an example was not made of Mexico. It was said—as it is said today—that Washington had to show its allies it had the strength to stand up to such threats.

But instead of sending in the Marines, Roosevelt proposed a diplomatic solution. We offered long-term credits to enable the Mexican government to compensate U.S. oil companies. The Mexicans immediately muted their anti-gringo rhetoric, and when the United States entered World War II, Mexico proved a staunch ally. Said Mexican author Carlos Fuentes, Roosevelt "did not beat history. He joined it."[14]

Roosevelt's imaginative response points up the fact that U.S. policy in the region has not always been one of intervention and intimidation, as is the consistent case with the Soviet Union and its neighbors. In all the missile-rattling rhetoric of the "East-West confrontation," that difference is too often forgotten. Also overlooked is this critical reality: the United States is a democracy; the Soviet Union is a tyranny. In the failure to emphasize these differences in Latin America, the United States has played the Russians' own game. Policy makers have also failed to realize the power of pragmatic idealism to sway the peoples of Latin America, where religion is deeply embedded in the culture.

In none of the Central American nations, including El Salvador and Nicaragua, is it too late to pursue democratic objectives. But the longer the United States waits, the fewer the options. Contrary to the belief of some policy makers that they can turn back the clock to the 1950s, when the State Department made and unmade Central American governments,[15] the historical momentum for change is now too strong to reverse, even with the massive intervention of U.S. troops. The question is whether the United States wants to be part of the process of change, even if it is revolutionary change, or deny the lessons of history. Twice before the United States failed to take the initiative—in 1959, when Fidel Castro came to power in Cuba, and in 1978 and early 1979, when the Sandinistas had not yet consolidated military supremacy in Nicaragua. Today another failed opportunity looms.

PART I. PEACE: THE PRECONDITION FOR DEMOCRATIC GROWTH IN CENTRAL AMERICA.

Even in the simplest of circumstances, the idea that money can solve everything is naive. To suggest that it can buy economic and political development in the middle of a war, as proposed by the Kissinger Commission, is nonsense: it is impossible to build when everything is being torn down.

Kissinger Commission Summary

In summary, the Kissinger Commission proposes an $8 billion, five-year aid package for Central America, including large increases in military aid, particularly for El Salvador, where it recommends $400 million in U.S. assistance over the next two years.[16] The Reagan administration is seeking congressional support for the aid proposals, but with U.S. public opinion opposed to further U.S. involvement in Central America,[17] it is questionable whether Congress will approve so huge an outlay –especially during an election year.

The essential weakness of the Kissinger report is that it was conceived in a U.S. political context, and Washington's realpolitik has nothing to say to the historic condition of starving peasants. Recommendations for economic assistance are not set within the framework of national needs but are thrown out, willy-nilly, in a mass of generalities. No attempt is made to explain how the Central Americans could make practical use of such aid, though it is clear that existing aid programs are ensnarled in bureaucratic red tape and corruption.[18]

Alliance for Progress

The report's worst flaw is its marriage of military and economic aid. That, too, was the principal failing of President Kennedy's Alliance for Progress, a policy that insisted on military aid to provide "stability" for economic development. In Central America such aid was earmarked primarily for training local armies in counterinsurgency techniques and for police programs supported by the Agency for International Development (AID). As amply documented,[19] such training reinforced the military's belief that any and all opposition to the status quo was Marxist-inspired and that the military were the chosen leaders to save their countries from communism. The RAND Corporation, a California think tank that advises both the State and Defense Departments, reported that U.S. military assistance programs "facilitate(d) preoccupation with military response to national security" and encouraged the belief that all rebellions in Latin America, even if necessary for social change, were bad by definition, with the result that Washington automatically defended reactionary or status quo governments from such violence.[20]

At the end of the Alliance decade, thousands of innocent Central Americans, mostly peasants, had died in counterinsurgency sweeps, and all attempts at a democratic opening in Guatemala, Nicaragua, El Salvador, and Honduras had been brutally repressed. The message from Washington was clear to both the extreme right and the extreme left: the United States, despite its reformist rhetoric, would always side with the region's reactionary forces. Proof could be seen in our country's rapidly dwindling interest in social and economic reforms once military control was assured. As pointed out in a dissenting note by Kissinger Commission member Robert S. Strauss, the "creation and/or preservation of pluralistic government depends as much or more on a basic restructuring of internal political institutions as on military assistance"[21]– essentially the same view held by the RAND Corporation more than a decade ago.

Whether U.S. economic assistance would actually be used for economic development may also be questioned, particularly in countries like Guatemala, El Salvador, and Honduras, where government for all practical purposes is run by the military. In times of war, when economic resources are concentrated on the battlefield, most economic aid is directed to that end. An example is the land reform program in El Salvador, which has suffered as much from a lack of resources as opposition from right-wing landowners.[22] Then too, the availability of huge sums of money to traditionally corrupt military institutions is an invitation to dishonesty, as shown by the thefts and payoffs among army officers in El Salvador and Honduras.[23] Consequently, were Congress to support the Kissinger Commission's economic aid proposals, it would be throwing good taxpayers' money after bad. There can be no economic or democratic growth in Central America until regional strife is ended, and this cannot be achieved until the United States abandons a military solution.

Though often cited by administration spokesmen as an example for Central America, the Marshall Plan succeeded in Europe precisely because post-war governments were at peace. They also had democratic institutions and development expertise on which to build, both rare commodities in Central America.

Any attempt to seek regional peace in Central America must be treated as a complex process. One of the errors in U.S. policy in Latin America has been to treat the region as a single unit, whereas there are important historical differences that distinguish each nation. Thus the process must be a "two-track" one in which local conflicts are treated separately, while at the same time the players interact at a regional level.

El Salvador

The lack of progress in talks between the opposition FMLN-FDR* on the one hand and the Salvadoran government and U.S. representatives on the other, shows how difficult dialogue will remain so long as armed hostilities continue. Neither side seriously regards the other's declared desire for peace when they are killing each other on the battlefield. For armed hostilities to cease, pressure is necessary from regional and international players. The three most important are the United States, Cuba, and Nicaragua; a fourth force, as yet undefined, may emerge from U.S. public opinion.

As the provider of more than $23 million a month in aid to the Salvadoran government and military, the United States holds a leverage so far not exercised. The war in El Salvador is not going well for the United States' allies, even with the increase in training, equipment, and money for the military. Morale is declining as the guerrillas increase in boldness, and it is now estimated that the FMLN controls up to one-third of the country. The guerrilla forces are well armed, in large part with U.S. weapons captured during battles with the Salvadoran army, and most military and political experts believe it is only a matter of time—though precisely how long is anyone's guess— before they gain military supremacy. Informed Central American sources claim the only reason the FMLN did not seize more territory in its last offensive was because it feared the United States would respond with massive military intervention. Consequently there are sound strategic reasons for the U.S. to support a halt in hostilities at this point: its allies are losing while their opponents are sufficiently wary of U.S. military power to be receptive to a truce.[24]

Of course there is the other alternative—sending in U.S. troops. But there is no political support in the United States for such an action (opinion polls are running four to one against further U.S. military involvement in Central America[25]). U.S. military intervention would also damage U.S. relations with the rest of Latin America, where economic and strategic interest are far more vital than in tiny, impoverished Salvador. Moreover, to succeed, the cost in money and lives would be high. Unlike Grenada, a U.S. invasion of El Salvador would not be a quick mop-up operation because the guerrillas have a large, battle-toughened army. And to hold its strategic gains, the United States would have to occupy the country for several years and deal with all the political and economic problems that occupation would surely bring.[26]

As shown by Nixon's rapprochement with China, the Reagan ad-

---

*The FMLN (Farabundo Marti Nation Liberation Front) represents five guerrilla groups fighting in El Salvador; the FDR (Democratic Revolutionary Front), is a broad coalition of civilian opposition including moderate to radical forces.

ministration is in a stronger political position to initiate a dialogue with the Salvadoran left than are the Democrats–if only public opinion and Congress can persuade the President of the need to negotiate. It is to everyone's advantage to tone down the rhetoric about who "lost" Nicaragua and who will be responsible for "losing" El Salvador since both Republican and Democratic administrations share responsibility for mistakes in Central America. What is more, the Central American countries are not ours to "lose" in any case. Neither party can gain from warmongering, for the American people are clearly concerned about survival in a nuclear war. Moreover, most Americans are so confused by the rhetoric on Central America that they don't even know which side the United States supports.[27] Were the realities addressed in cool, clear language, policy makers might be able to deal with the issues, without worrying about the loss of public confidence. It is, after all, the test of statesmanship to rise above the crowd to see the real stakes and longer-term consequences.

The Mexican government has been attempting to persuade President Reagan of the need for such vision, so far unsuccessfully. Mexico believes it has more to lose from the ongoing political convulsions in Central America, which could overflow its southern borders, than from a left-wing government in El Salvador. Likewise, the United States has no important economic, financial or strategic interest at stake in El Salvador, whereas a regional war could threaten important U.S. interest in the Panama Canal and Mexico's oil fields. "Each country has its own requirements, its own institutions, traditions, and history," said Mexico's Foreign Minister Bernardo Sepulveda. "To say that a change, a revolution in one country, will precipitate upheaval in all its neighbors in succession is not an expression of sympathy with any of them. It is a statement of contempt."[28]

A political, rather than a military course could be undertaken in El Salvador if U.S. military support were suspended. But the principal arguments cited against a suspension of aid must be confronted. Those arguments are:

1. It would encourage Salvador's extreme right to take a fortress-like attitude by responding with a bloodbath.

2. The United States would be abandoning the country to the Marxists.

The first argument ignores the fact that a bloodbath already is in progress: some 40,000 people have died since 1979, and 10 percent of the population has been displaced.[29] While there are some die-hard zealots in the civilian and military right, it is not at all clear that the majority of the Salvadoran army is disposed to a heroic but pointless end. On the contrary, the record shows that many officers are more concerned with personal aggrandizement and the institution's survival. At the same time, a number of officers have shown themselves prepared to consider negotiations. In October 1982, for example, when the FMLN called for "dialogue without preconditions," a group of army field commanders circulated a letter criticizing the government's rejection of the suggestion, pointing out that it was easy for others to refuse dialogue from the comfort, luxury, and safety of the capital.[30]

The answer to the second argument is that, barring U.S. military intervention, the guerrillas will win in any case. But, if they can be brought to negotiations through a military truce, other factors and groups may influence the situation to prevent the emergence of a hardline Marxist regime. American analysts who lived in Southeast Asia point to the parallel with the war in Vietnam when Washington insisted on the whole pie and ended up without a crumb. In a civil war between the extreme left and extreme right, as in El Salvador, the only way moderates can make themselves heard is through a coalition.[31]

On the other side of the question, the Cubans and Nicaraguans already have signalled that they are prepared to encourage the guerrillas to accept a ceasefire. For purely pragmatic reasons—or the survival of their own revolutions—the Castro and Sandinista governments favor initiatives which will reduce U.S. pressure on them. The U.S. invasion of Grenada was seen as a frightening precedent for possible future scenarios in the region.

In the aftermath, war fever gripped Nicaragua and Cuba. Trenches were dug throughout Nicaragua in the expectation of imminent U.S. bombing. Equally fearful of a U.S. military invasion, the Salavadoran guerrillas have repeatedly stated their willingness to negotiate.[32]

Political and military strategists believe it is possible to establish a truce based on existing zones of control, with a regional or international peace force to insure that neither side attempts to extend military influence. Although the Organization of American States has been suggested as a possible police force, its record in earlier regional conflicts has made it suspect as a U.S. tool in the eyes of Central American insurgents. Another group perceived as more neutral would be a better choice. One such is the Contadora* group comprised of Mexico, Panama, Venezuela and Colombia. The Contadoras have been actively seeking a negotiated settlement in Central America. Another choice might be the United Nations.

As suggested in a November, 1980, "dissent paper" believed to reflect the views of critical analysts in the State Department, CIA, and other government agencies, a truce could lead to a Zimbabwe-style solution.[33] Just as the British intervened to end the conflict in Rhodesia by recognizing the left, the United States could recognize the FDR as a legitimate force in negotiations. While a regional or interna-

*So called because the peace group first met on the Panamanian island of Contadora.

18

tional peace force would guarantee the physical safety of the negotiators, impartiality would need to be insured by local, regional, and international representatives to provide balance. The archbishop of San Salvador, Monsignor Arturo Rivera y Damas, is one example of a local leader respected for his impartial support of human rights. Regional representatives obviously would include the United States and, as a counterweight, a Latin American country acceptable to the FDR and the guerrillas (i.e., Mexico). Other Latin American and possibly European nations and/or well-known international figures might also be party to the negotiations. This group could further guarantee the functioning of an interim government.

Such negotiations would take considerable time and require certain conditions, including a "purging" of the most intransigent members of the military and the guerrillas to guarantee that talks are not subverted by continuing hostilities. This could be achieved in two ways, both of which would have lasting benefits for the country.

The first would establish a system of impartial courts—with the aid of an internationally recognized body of jurists—to bring to trial those accused of the torture and murder of civilians. (Argentina is doing this under the reformist civilian government of President Raul Alfonsin.) Reports by Salvador's Catholic Church and human rights organiza-tions show that most torture and murder have been the work of right-wing death squads connected to the security forces.[34] In itself, the threat of justice would encourage such elements to leave the country. More important, it would establish the supremacy of law while discrediting the future use of terror as a political weapon. The lack of judicial independence has been one of the fundamental weaknesses in Central American politics, and establishing such courts would contribute to a system of checks and balances. Just as Argentina's newly independent courts have served as a warning to other military regimes in South America by trying officials accused of murder, such a system might discourage atrocities in other Central American countries, particularly Guatemala, where the military has used death squads to wipe out the political center.[35] U.S. support of such courts would reinforce that warning while demonstrating our country's commitment to justice and the rule of law.

As in Argentina, guerrillas accused of such crimes would be subject to the same penalties as the military. However, a second initiative would also be necesary to isolate the most intransigent members of both groups. Support must be given the more moderate and pragmatic forces within the different factions. Contrary to the black-and-white picture painted in the United States, neither the military nor the FMLN-FDR is a homogenous group. Under legal, political, and financial pressures, extremists in the military could be forced to give way to reformist officers uncompromised by the taint of the death squads.[36] Pressure could also be exercised by the United States (i.e., through the promise or withholding of aid and trade commitments) in support of the more pragmatic members of the FMLN-FDR, which includes different political currents.

While no one has suggested that the FMLN's leaders can be converted to espousing a U.S. political and economic system, a U.S. policy that emphasizes the reality of Central America—thus recognizing and appealing to nationalist sentiments —could dilute the hard-line Marxism of some guerrilla leaders. The reality is that El Salvador is located in the U.S. sphere of influence, and thus, no matter what the ideology of the government, it must depend on the United States for trade and aid. By repeated refusal to supply large quantities of aid or arms to either Nicaragua or the Salvadoran guerrillas, the Soviet Union has shown its reluctance to get bogged down in another economic swamp like Cuba. The Sandinista government in Nicaragua recognized that reality—which is another reason it would like to improve relations with the United States.[37]

Obviously there are risks in a diplomatic approach. But the risks are small compared with those inherent in the U.S. government's current course. That course, if followed to its logical conclusion, will end in the large-scale use of U.S. troops to put down the Salvadoran rebellion at considerable loss in lives for Americans as well as Salvadorans.

Negotiations would also aid the democratic left-of-center, the size and strength of which may be greater than generally assumed. Many Salvadorans who have provided noncombatant aid to the guerrillas (i.e. giving them food) belonged to such popular non-Marxist organizations as the unions and peasant federations that were forced to go underground after the reformist junta fell in 1980 (see page 2). Most had ties to the Catholic Church, and a number grew out of the church's grassroots organization work. Based on such ties and their earlier political positions, most would not vote for a hard-line Marxist government in free elections. Instead, they would likely favor some form of Christian socialism or a Social Democratic style of government. During the most recent demonstrations of their strength, in late 1979 and early 1980, these organizations drew crowds of up to 300,000 Salvadorans, even though roadblocks were set up to prevent peasants from joining demonstrations and participants were threatened with violence. Those 300,000 people represent approximately 20 percent of the electorate, and while some have since been killed, they and their organizations still offer the possibility of a democratic alternative to the guerrillas. A large number of other Salvadorans have opted for the political center, as shown by the 1982 constituent assembly elections in which the Christian Democrats won more than one-third of the vote.[38] All these people–and possibly many others who have not dared to express a political opinion –suggest a potentially strong political center and center-left which the United States should support. They are another reason for negotiations, for if the conflict in El Salvador is settled by military force, military leaders will dominate any post-war government. Impartial Central Americans believe that under such circumstances concessions to democracy would be minimal and that the government would be much more dogmatic than the Sandinistas in Nicaragua.

The key to negotiations in El Salvador is recognizing that there is no quick fix; that talks among the various factions undoubtedly will be prolonged and difficult.[39] On the other hand, there is an advantage to a slower process, since it would give local democratic forces time to regroup and grow. A thorough public discussion of the country's problems might also lead to a social consensus important for genuinely free elections and for post-war economic development.

Nicaragua

While complex, the issues involving regional peace and Nicaragua are considerably more straight-forward than negotiations in El Salvador. They center on the following conditions:

1. An end to the CIA's covert support of the counterrevolutionaries (contras) making war on Nicaragua.*

2. Support for the Contadora groups' 21-point peace program to end hostilities between Nicaragua and its neighbors.[40]

3. Nonagression treaties between Nicaragua and its neighbors.

4. Nonagression treaties between Nicaragua and the United States.

To achieve these goals, certain safeguards would have to be provided, perhaps by a regional association like the Contadora group. These would include commitments by Nicaragua and its neighbors to stop the military buildup by placing a freeze on further arms acquisitions or any increase in military forces, the removal of foreign military advisers and combat officers, the elimination of all arms flows in support of revolutionary or counterrevolutionary forces in neighboring countries, the refusal of asylum to such groups, and a prohibition against the establishment of foreign military bases in the area.

A regional or international police force could insure that the signatories of the treaties adhere to these

---

*Also proposed by two members of the Kissinger Commision, Henry G. Cisneros and Carlos F. Diaz-Alejandro, in a dissenting view against the majority's support for the Reagan position.

terms. Given the sophistication of U.S. surveillance technology, it would be very difficult for Nicaragua to break the treaty terms and not be found out, with the certain consequence of international condemnation. Moreover, if a promise of U.S. nonaggression were accompanied by one of improved trade and economic relations, the Sandinista government would have all the more reason to adhere to such conditions. Indeed, it is in the economic sphere that the United States holds the best cards, and it is here, rather than in the military arena, that it can do most to encourage political democracy in Nicaragua (see Part II).

The treaties could also include a framework for a second round of regional negotiations–this time for a gradual disarmament once tensions had relaxed.

The precondition for a negotiated peace settlement is an end to U.S. funding, training, and arming of the *contra* rebels on Nicaragua's northern and southern borders. Contrary to the Reagan administration's original assertion that the aim of the operation was to "interdict" Nicaraguan arms shipments to the Salvadoran rebels, it has been amply demonstrated by congressional investigations–and the administration's own admissions–that the purpose is to overthrow the Sandinista government.[41]* Not only

is that aim in contravention of U.S.-Latin American treaties, it also ignores the constitutional responsibility of Congress to grant the authority to wage war in whatever disguise. It further implies that the United States has the right to choose the form of government in Nicaragua. At the same time, the use of Honduras and Costa Rica as launching pads for the counter-revolution has undermined those countries' democratic institutions and increased the odds of a war between Nicaragua and Honduras. Such a war would likely involve U.S. forces stationed in Honduras, posing the possibility of direct U.S. military intervention in Nicaragua, since the Pentagon itself admits that neither the *contras* nor the Honduran armed forces alone are capable of defeating the Sandinistas.

If a successful U.S. invasion of El Salvador is problematic, the odds in Nicaragua are far worse. Unlike El Salvador, Nicaragua suffered a long period of Marine occupation in the early part of this century, and Nicaraguans will never forget that the hated Somoza dynasty was imposed on them by the U.S. State Department. Having sacrificed 40,000 lives, many of them children, to overthrow Somoza, they will not easily suffer the imposition of rule by the *contras*, even at the point of U.S. bayonets, since most of the *contras* were members of Somoza's

*U.S. hostility also contradicts the Kissinger Commission's use of social and economic reforms to improve the masses' standard of living, for the only country in the Central American crisis area to have done just that is Nicaragua. According to a report by the Overseas Development Council, a private Washington-based organization, Nicaragua notched up a 16-point gain in its "physical quality of life index," with notable improvements in literacy, infant mortality, and life expectancy.

22

brutal National Guard.[42]

Nicaragua is both larger than El Salvador and of more complex terrain, and to fight a guerrilla war against virtually the entire population would be logistically difficult, unacceptably expensive, and very costly in U.S. lives. Augusto Cesar Sandino, an earlier guerrilla fighter and Nicaragua's national hero, demonstrated how a small force of dedicated Nicaraguans can hold down U.S. military forces for years—thus portending that the United States could once again be mired in a long, debilitating struggle like Vietnam, with no guarantee of final success. Any suggestion that the Nicaraguans would welcome U.S. forces as liberating heroes should be dismissed out of hand. As in El Salvador, nationalism is the engine behind the Nicaraguan revolution; and no matter how much they may grumble about the Sandinistas, the one thing that would instantly unite Nicaraguans is U.S. intervention.

Military intervention would almost certainly lead to a regionalization of the conflict, bringing armed brigades from the Latin South American nations. There would also be a certain backlash against U.S. industries throughout Latin America and a threat to the Panama Canal. Not only would the United States invite near unanimous condemnation from Latin America and Europe, it would also escalate the confrontation between East and West—the very thing Washington claims it wants to prevent.

A winding down of the *contra* campaign, on the other hand, would hasten the negotiation of verifiable treaties to end hostilities. The treaties in turn would promote an atmosphere of peace in which military influence could be reduced to the advantage of civilian institutions, particularly in Honduras and Nicaragua. And the reestablishment of peace would enable these countries to devote scarce resources to the rebuilding of their economies, all of which are in serious straits.[43] A return to peace would also enable the United States to forge a more coherent regional policy, replacing crisis management with a better informed, more flexible approach to dealing with the serious problems looming on the horizon. Those looming problems include the possible repudiation of foreign debt by the largest Latin American client states of U.S. banks.

Cuba

To a large extent, U.S. animosity toward Nicaragua reflects the inheritance of a long, often illogical feud with Nicaragua's ally, Cuba. As with Nicaragua, the Eisenhower and Kennedy administrations refused to consider a diplomatic approach to Fidel Castro and helped push Cuba into the arms of the Soviets. On several occasions (i.e., talks with the Sandinista leadership and, earlier, with Chile's Socialist President Salvador Allende) Castro has lamented his country's over-

23

dependence on one of the super-powers. Carlos Fuentes, one of Latin America's most perceptive writers, has warned that, "By refusing to talk to Cuba, (Washington) not only weakens Cuba and the United States, but strengthens the Soviet Union."[44]

Wayne Smith, a former State Department expert on Cuba, has pointed out that Cuba is not the only country in the world with which the United States differs, yet with most of the other nations we still manage differences "through normal diplomatic channels." Said Smith: "Ironically, U.S. relations are better with the Soviet Union, its principal adversary, than with the USSR's small Caribbean associates."[45]

This contradictory behavior can be traced to the United States' historical distrust of nationalism in other countries, particularly those in its own "backyard," and to a sense of cultural superiority. Many Americans still think their country selflessly liberated Cuba from Spain. They do not realize that the Cubans never looked on it as liberation, because the United States has repeatedly intervened in their affairs, and sometimes with military force. Antagonisms reached an historical high over the missile crisis of 1962–and after the United States' failed invasion. But in the intervening years there have been no further threats to U.S. security, as evidenced by unimpeded U.S. shipping and military movements in the Caribbean.

Given the advanced technology of nuclear weaponry and intercontinental air and sea delivery, the Soviet Union does not need a Cuban base to launch an attack on the United States, Panama or Mexico. Moreover, in any nuclear scenario Cuba would be merely a part of a larger war between the United States and the Soviet Union that might originate in Europe or the Middle East. (It is often forgotten that the largest foreign base on Cuba–Guantanamo–belongs to the United States.) As to the claim that Cuba is fomenting subversion throughout Latin America, history repeatedly has proved that such efforts fail unless local conditions are as ripe for insurrection as they were in Nicaragua. Even the Reagan administration has not suggested that Castro orchestrated that rebellion. The U:S. invasion of Grenada.showed that Cuba does not have the capability to rush to the aid of its friends. Indeed, Castro himself has tried to make this reality understood by the Sandinistas.

Unfortunately, 25 years of antagonism has produced a mindset in the United States that is incapable of seeing how trade and diplomacy could drive a wedge between Cuba and the Soviet Union. The tragedy is that the same attitudes now cloud Washington's relations with Nicaragua, although Nicaragua is a much more pluralistic society than Cuba. At this juncture, Nicaragua neither needs nor deserves the kind of ignorant and arrogant treatment that makes enemies of potential friends.

PART II. DEMOCRATIC GROWTH: ORGANIZATIONS AND METHODS

The underlying premise of the following analysis of possibilities for democratic growth in Central America is that military solutions must be abandoned for political and diplomatic initiatives, including new approaches to aid and trade.

Neighborhood and Community Organizations

Despite the facade of legality, most Central American nations are not participatory societies. To understand that is to avoid a good deal of anguish—and mistaken policy decisions—over such failed illusions as elections, for elections often have no meaning in that cultural context. As El Salvador, Guatemala, Honduras, and Panama have shown, elections are frequently rigged. Often the illiterate masses are simply herded to the polls, like so many cattle, to vote for the choice of the local landowner or military commander.

The issue, then, must focus on basics—on those rural and urban community groups that traditionally have exercised a form of ad hoc democracy in local decisions. If there are any parallels in the United States, they are early ones, like the New England town meetings, rather than electronic voting and mass media campaigns. At this stage in Central America's political development, it matters less who is president or how he was elected than what input local residents have in the decision making process. These groups are building blocks in a slow process in overcoming centuries of anti-democratic traditions. If those traditions are not overcome, Central America will always be ruled by tyrannies of the right or the left.

Religion is one of the most important cultural links to neighborhood solidarity in Central America. In El Salvador, Honduras, Nicaragua, Guatemala, and Panama, the harbingers of change at the grassroots level were not guerrillas but Catholic priests and nuns. In the 1960s, they began working with small groups of poor peasants and urban workers in the formation of base communities. In their sense of solidarity, these base communities are similar to the primitive Christian communities of the early Roman church, but they are also deeply rooted in the Central American culture. For many poor people they offer the first experience with democracy—the opportunity to state an opinion publicly, engage in debate, and participate in a voting procedure in which the majority's decision is respected. But the greatest strength of the communities is their religious foundation. In a fatalistic culture in which the people have for centuries been led to believe that God is on the side of the rich, the communities offer the liberating lesson that God has always been on the side of the poor.

Out of the communities have grown labor unions and peasant federations, slum associations, cooperatives, and mothers' clubs, the intermediate groups so sorely lacking in Central America. During the 1970s, the communities were the backbone of rural protest, but as insurrection swept the region they were either drawn into the revolution, as in Nicaragua and El Salvador, or severely repressed, as in Guatemala. Nevertheless, the foundations remain. Indeed, one of the primary reasons pluralism has survived in Nicaragua is the influence of religion. (Despite divisions in the Nicaraguan church over the degree of support or opposition to the Sandinista regime, most of the population thinks of itself as Christian *and* revolutionary. Base community leaders say they do not identify with the revolution because of the Sandinistas' ideology but because it responds to the biblical "option for the poor."[45]

The network of hundreds of base communities also reflects the political culture of Central America, which is rooted in loyalty to neighborhood—village or *barrio*. Such loyalties were evident in the Nicaraguans' struggle against Somoza, when neighbors joined together to make weapons or provide logistical support for the guerrillas. Today the revolution is remembered not by massive monuments to the war dead, but by the streets named after the local citizens who sacrificed in its behalf.

Political Pluralism: The Experiment in Nicaragua

Since the revolution, most Nicaraguans have joined such community organizations as cooperatives or neighborhood block committees. Political pluralism will depend on the extent to which these groups are able to develop freely and demand an accounting of the Sandinista leadership, not only on community issues (which already have significant local input) but on national questions liable to affect them, particularly in the economic sphere.[47] Constituent assembly elections are scheduled for early 1985, and most observers, including the American ambassador, feel the Sandinistas will win a majority. But while the elections will strengthen the revolution by proving its popular support, they will not substantially alter the current power structure since the same people now running the government will head the Sandinista slate.

Within the leadership ideological tendencies range from moderate to extreme left, and foreign and Nicaraguan sources stress the importance of *not* pursuing policies which, in effect, support the extremists. Hostile measures like the *contra* war and the suspension of U.S. aid, for example, have forced

26

the Sandinistas to seek help from the Socialist bloc. A case in point was the January bombing of Nicaragua's northern borders by *contra*-Honduran forces. The bombing occurred just when the government was to open the election campaign, and the Sandinistas abruptly announced that the electoral process had been postponed indefinitely because of the attacks. Under pressure from the moderates and the revolution's Social Democratic friends in Europe and Latin America, the government changed its mind a few days later. But the see-saw showed how *contra* attacks can strengthen the hard-line Marxists in government who see no advantage in free elections.[48]

Support for the moderates would encourage the "political space" needed by community groups to mature and to establish a new tradition of pluralism. Like most Central Americans, the Nicaraguans have been conditioned by decades of dictatorship not to question or criticize. The war atmosphere caused by the *contra* attacks is not conducive to dialogue since everyone's efforts are concentrated on staying alive*; hence the CIA's war on Nicaragua not only destroys lives and property but also undermines the chances for democracy.

Agrarian Reform

As elsewhere in Central America, a key issue in the democratic process is agrarian reform since the majority of the people live in rural poverty. But a war atmosphere is not conducive to reform, as witness the lack of progress in the land distribution program in El Salvador. But peace is only one condition for success. Equally important is the participation of the local populace in the formulation of such a reform. The failed agrarian reforms sponsored by the Alliance for Progress and more recently by the plan for El Salvador drawn up by the AFL-CIO's American Institute for Free Labor Development are evidence that the imposition of foreign, or more precisely U.S., theories of justice in the countryside is resented by the local populace.[†] Moreover, such theories frequently do not work because foreign technicians do not understand local cultural and economic realities and thus misdirect the emphases. Land redistribution is only one element in the complex issue of agrarian reform, for this issue also touches on the

---

*Nicaraguan health workers say the most commonly reported illnesses among adults are psychosomatic and attribute the problem to tensions arising from the *contra* war.

---

†The Institute's documented ties to the CIA and role as Trojan Horse in labor disputes with U.S. corporations have caused widespread resentment among Central American workers, who see it as an arm of "U.S. imperialism." Had the Institute genuinely identified with the workers' cause, the region's labor movement would be stronger, more democratic, and more pro-U.S. today. (Penny Lernoux, *Cry of the People* [Penguin: New York, 1982], pp. 118, 156, 211-213, 226, 238, 310.)

urban cost of living, inflation, foreign exchange earnings, and a host of other factors. Moreover, land ownership is meaningless for the rural poor unless it is accompanied by higher productivity and higher incomes, which in turn mean different priorities for the national government. Thus to be both realistic and democratic, agrarian reform must take into account all the different groups and interests affected.[49]

Based on the peasants' experience in Central America, the most successful approach to democratic growth in rural areas is through a cooperative movement, provided, of course, that the cooperatives are not persecuted and receive a measure of financial and technical help. In most of Guatemala and El Salvador, the present possibility of foreign support for cooperatives is severely limited by insecure conditions in the countryside. But even in the other Central American countries the need for outside aid is not excessive. Rural leaders say they do not need foreigners to teach them how to organize themselves; they also point out that when donations are excessively large the donor usually wants a say in how the cooperative is organized and operated. Instead, they suggest Spanish-speaking technicians who are able to "fix things" and obtain the means of "fixing." For example, most rural areas in Central America use U.S. farm machinery. If a cooperative has

only one tractor and the tractor breaks down, there probably will be no spare parts or mechanic to fix it. Small as this detail may seem, it has severely hampered agricultural production in countries like Honduras and Nicaragua. The right kind of technical help is also needed in the marketing of rural goods, which include artisan work as well as food produce.

In addition, groups of cooperatives usually need an "advocate," at least in the early stages of formation. An advocate is someone with a certain authority who is able to get things done, usually by badgering government officials or serving as a go-between. In Central America, foreign priests and nuns often fill this role, but there is need for many more such advocates. The prime considerations for usefulness are a skill, a connection with an international organization that will provide backup supplies (i.e., medicine or spare tires), and a willingness to listen to what the people want instead of imposing preconceived notions.

Like labor unions in the cities, cooperatives are the first step toward political expression at the regional and national level. But those who work with such groups caution that this is a long and frustrating process in which the momentum can be set back by local squabbles or generalized repression. El Salvador provides but one example.

Private Aid

As observed in the Introduction, Central America does not need huge sums of aid and guns from the United States so much as it needs a willingness to help the Central Americans along a path of their own choosing. Some of the best mechanisms for such help are private and multilateral. The overwhelming U.S. presence in Central America since World War II has made many of its official aid programs suspect, particularly since they were later shown to have been used for political purposes. (The Salvadoran agrarian reform's close similarity to the United States' rural pacification program in Vietnam is a case in point.) Private efforts usually do not bear such taint, particularly if they are part of a regional or international project. What is more, the Americans who participate in such programs are often better ambassadors of good will than embassy personnel, whose job is to represent their government's point of view. Official U.S. aid programs should be directed not by government agencies but by private religious organizations, farmers' associations, educational foundations and universities, labor unions, cooperatives, chambers of commerce, citizens' and legal organizations, sports federations, or the many intermediate groups that make up the social fabric of U.S. democracy. These organizations relate more effectively to the needs of intermediate groups in Central America, and an inter-change of ideas and people would contribute greatly to an improvement in U.S.-Central American relations. Moreover, the record of private initiative has proved infinitely more successful—and less costly—than government programs.

Private U.S. foundations can play an important role in bringing together diverse groups to help the Central Americans and by providing modest financing to support those efforts. The infrastructure for such aid already exists in many parts of Central America through U.S. Catholic and Protestant organizations working in the area. To achieve more than a passing ripple effect, however, foundations must recognize two conditions. The first is that success can only be achieved through long-term commitment to a given project, for there is no quick fix in the cultural context of Central America. To begin a project and abandon it in a year or so is more of a disservice than to have done nothing. The second is the active involvement of community groups in the foreign financing of local projects; they should monitor how the aid is actually used through a system of checks and balances. This is particularly important to help counter bureaucratic corruption in government supported aid projects. Giving community groups a greater say in financial matters increases their stake in the success of the project and the likelihood of loan repayment if that is a condition. Such participation can also lead to more efficient aid administration. (The community is in a better position to know whether it will be best served by the supply of spare parts, the loan of a technician or funds to buy local materials.) Finally, such co-administration encourages the people to take pride in running their own affairs, instead of being patronized by a foreigner, and pride is the beginning of political assertiveness.

In the category of foreign givers there is yet another group. These are "Good Samaritans," the people who give their time and sometimes risk their lives to show solidarity with the Central Americans. The many private U.S. groups that have visited Central America out of concern to see and understand the reality first-hand are so considered by the Central Americans, who understand such gestures as a protest against current Washington policy. This is particularly so in Nicaragua, where peace groups have traveled to the war-torn northern border at considerable risk to themselves in protest against the CIA's warmaking role there.

A Sample Aid Program

A West German aid expert calculated that a five-year aid program for Nicaragua would not cost more than $40 million or involve more than 60 foreign technicians. Though seemingly modest in scope, the effects would multiply throughout society, he said. He also maintained that the program's lack of grandiose pretensions would not pose a political problem, as the United States' land reform program has done in El Salvador.[50]

His shopping list:

1. Mechanics and spare parts to repair tractors, trucks, and the buses (so critically needed for public transport), and to teach the people how to use machinery without ruining it.

2. Technicians to organize and maintain transport systems.

3. Agronomists who can help teach the cooperatives how to administer their enterprises, request loans, apply elemental accounting, and insure a fair share of profits and losses.

4. Experts in reforestation, soil erosion, and water conservation and the means to undertake such projects.

5. Planning experts who can help government agencies, particularly in statistics and computer use.[51]

In assessing the basic nature of Nicaragua's needs, it must be remembered that this country does not even have a population census or any reliable yardstick for measuring the GNP. A Belgian doctor pointed up the dramatic impact of this lack of basic information. Having helped establish elementary

30

paramedic groups in northern Nicaragua, she and her group were stymied because they had no idea how many people lived in the area or what the principal medical problems were. Consequently, officials in the capital had no way of knowing what health priorities to assign to the area.[52]

Foreign health workers in Nicaragua also made an observation that applies to any aid program anywhere in Central America. They said such programs should not be so sophisticated as to be useless.

Modern medical equipment and hospitals, for example, often are beyond the financial means of the Central Americans. Hence there is no point in constructing an expensively equipped installation if it is going to fall apart in a year or two, or need constant infusions of foreign aid and personnel. Hence the emphasis should be on preventive medicine, which is relatively cheap, easier to administer and teach, and more adaptable to local conditions at this time.

A Larger Economic Framework

Grassroots initiatives need a larger economic and political framework. The political preconditions have been outlined in Part I in respect to the reestablishment of regional peace and the need for policies of nonaggression. But to insure that peace yields more than a return to pre-1979 conditions, new political and economic initiatives are necessary. As pointed out by Kissinger Commission member Carlos F. Diaz-Alejandro, in a dissenting note on the commission's conclusions,[53] the carrot in the Central American political process depends less on economic and military aid than on the promise of trade concessions. These concessions involve serious decisions affecting not only U.S. relations with Central America but with the entire Third World.

All the Central American economies are in serious trouble because of a recession which has reached depression levels in many parts of Latin America.[54] Five of the Central American nations have also been adversely affected by regional wars that have destroyed production and trade and forced governments to earmark scarce income for military purposes. An enlightened U.S. policy would seek to use economic need to promote democratic concessions in favor of pluralism. Thus, instead of reducing Nicaragua's U.S. sugar quota, as the Reagan administration has done, the carrot approach would offer to increase the quota in exchange for a democratic gesture. One such gesture might be the establishment of an independent judiciary, a democratic check lacking in the Sandinista government. Similarly, the promise of a larger coffee quota for El Salvador might be injected into a discussion on agrarian reform. U.S. trade concessions would also help Honduras and Costa Rica. At the same time, all the Central American countries would benefit from the U.S. Treasury's support of a renegotiation of the region's foreign debt with U.S. banks in order to provide lower interest rates and longer periods of repayment. The one country that seems immune to carrot or stick is Guatemala, where, according to Amnesty International, a long line of military regimes has established one of the world's worst records for human rights violations. But while there may be little hope of an improvement in the near future, the carrot could at least be tried there, too. An increase in the U.S. coffee quota on which Guatemala's economy depends is one option.

U.S. trade and aid could also promote regional economic integration through multilateral agricultural and industrial enterprises. These, in turn, might help resuscitate the moribund Central American free trade association. But to insure that the benefits of development are spread throughout society, these endeavors should not be monopolized by a small elite in partnership with multi-national corporations as they were during the earlier trade association. While foreign investment is needed in Central America, new entrepreneurial groups must also be encouraged as a complement to the grassroots organizations by giving these democratic structures a solid economic underpinning. An example might be a regional federation of banana producer and marketing cooperatives that would both increase the workers' income and managerial skills and contribute to community development. (The principal reason such cooperatives have not succeeded to date is lack of government and/or because of government repression.)

Economic Barriers

While trade concessions have frequently been proposed as a solution to the problems of Central America and the Caribbean, they rarely add up to much because the issues are complex and U.S. administrations are not disposed to deal with them. For example, U.S. quotas for Central American commodities invariably run into the problem of international commodity pacts and the need for one country to sacrifice in order for another to gain. Behind that dilemma is the even thornier one of the price which consumer countries (i.e., the United States) are prepared to pay the producers. Although Third World nations have long complained that the terms of trade consistently work to their disadvantage (more and more sacks of coffee are necessary to buy the same tractor), neither the United States nor its allies in Europe and Japan have been disposed to listen. Similarly, any relaxation of the terms of debt repayment by the Central American countries immediately brings up the entire question of Third World debt, because concessions to one country will be demanded by others. Thus, while the answers to Central America's economic problems may seem obvious, the solutions inevitably are mixed up with the more complex questions confronting North-South relations. Although suggestions for new initiatives have been made by many international work groups (i.e., the Brandt Commission), thus far the political will to test them has been lacking.

PART III: AN ACTION PLAN

The following points outline possible steps that can be taken to help end hostilities in Central America and promote initiatives for democratic growth. They are based on a two-pronged strategy of (a) ensuring executive accountability by, among other things, providing Congress and others with non-partisan policy studies and analyses of issues necessary to permit informed policy debate, and (b) a network of private organizations which, while not necessarily able to change government policy in Central America, can demonstrate by their protest of policy and their empathy with the Central American people that there are *alternative* American positions on the question. Given the reluctance of many in government to risk a new approach to the Central American dilemma,* private groups will probably play a more important role. Hence the action plan begins with "b."

1. *Basic Information.* Many American groups support private aid programs in Central America and educational campaigns in the United States. But while there may be an informal tradeoff of information, no comprehensive assessment of who is doing what and where is available. Such information is impor-

tant to avoid overlap, to pool resources, and to improve networking. Similarly, there is no central information office to provide concerned individuals and groups with basic resource materials and the links to other organizations. Consequently, different groups are using scarce resources to repeat the work of others (i.e., basic information packets), when more could be achieved by sharing the tasks. Information centralization does not mean that any group will dominate another, but only that they will cooperate in letting others know what they are doing. Such a center should be located in Washington, where several organizations concerned with Central America already are headquartered. This would also facilitate congressional lobbying efforts. Financing could be supplied by a foundation.†

2. *Networking in Central America.* Such information can facilitate the people-to-people programs outlined in Part II. A number of U.S. organizations, particularly religious and humanitarian, have had long experience in working at the community level in Central America. Their contacts with peasants and lower class urban neighborhoods have enabled them to establish a social infrastruc-

---

*As candidly admitted by New Jersey's Congressman Robert G. Torricelli, the problem is, who will be blamed for losing Central America? "We may all be blamed. Those who promoted a policy that has alienated the people of Latin America from this country, and those of us who didn't stop it." ("Concerning U.S. Military and Paramilitary Operations in Nicaragua," Markup before the Committee on Foreign Affairs, House of Representatives [Washington: U.S. Government Printing Office, May 18, June 6 and 7, 1983], p. 23.)

†As this paper goes to press, efforts of this kind are underway by The Central American Education Project in Washington, DC.

ture upon which private aid groups new to the region could build. Such cooperation has two advantages. First, grassroots groups have more confidence in outsiders if they are connected to foreigners who have worked with them and whom they trust. Second, knowledge of the local reality can help newcomers avoid mistakes (i.e., trying to organize a button factory when the people want a fishing cooperative). Religious groups working with base communities emphasize the importance of allowing the people to decide which project they want; otherwise, they will not succeed. Moreover, community decision-making contributes to democratic growth.

3. *U.S. Promotion.* Publicity should be given to these programs at the community level in the United States. For example, a people-to-people project sponsored by a parish in the United States should be promoted not only at the parish level but in the larger community as well. The aim of such publicity is not so much to obtain funding as to encourage a personal identification with the Central Americans whom the project is helping. Commitment to a cause is usually greater when seen in terms of individual needs, and the more Americans know about the conditions in a particular village or *barrio*, the more likely they are to seek information on the wider Central American picture.

Publicity should stress that such projects are not charity, that we are not doing these things just because we think it wrong for children to starve, but because we need to reaffirm our beliefs in America's democratic principles. This is an act of conscience.

The same point should be made in Central America—and has been made by the many Americans visiting or working in Nicaragua who stress that their presence is not only a humanitarian gesture but also a deliberate alternative to Washington's support of the *contra* war. The goodwill inherent in such gestures is important for future U.S. relations with Central America, for it will remain as a testament to American principles in spite of an unprincipled U.S. policy. Unlike Vietnam, which is geographically distant from the United States and has spun off into its own geopolitical orbit, the Central Americans are our neighbors and will continue to have cultural and economic ties with the United States. The empathy now shown by private American groups will play a significant role in maintaining those ties.

4. *One Message With One Voice.* The simpler the message, the easier it is to get across. Instead of discussion about complex political issues in Nicaragua, for example, U.S. support groups should emphasize four straight-forward points. The first three appeal to self-interest; the fourth, to the basic humanity of Americans:

a. We do not want our young people killed in a remote jungle, in a war most Americans do not support or understand, and therefore we

35

should insist on peace initiatives. (The first real interest in Central America shown by the American public occurred in response to the murder of four American religious women in El Salvador.)

b. Wars cost taxpayers money. The United States has many needs and problems at home without adding to the burden by engaging in long and ultimately unsuccessful wars in Central America.

c. The return of peace in Central America will reduce the refugee flow into the United States, thereby safeguarding U.S. jobs.[55]

d. It is not right to support a government that tortures and murders innocent people, including Americans (El Salvador), nor is it right to finance, train, and supply a CIA army to overthrow another government (Nicaragua) which came to power through a popular revolution.[56]

One Voice. More networking needs to be done among the different sectors concerned with Central America in order to speak with a single voice. These include religious, human rights, labor union, and minority groups. Many are still divided over priorities or do not see the importance of linking up with other sectors. Thus, more effort is needed to show how all have a stake in Central America (i.e., focusing on racial discrimination, women's subservient role, repression of trade unions). In finding a common ground in the Central American debate, they might also discover new ways of approaching shared problems in the United States. This is an area where foundations and religious and human rights groups can make a contribution by offering their offices as go-between and by showing how, tactically, it is important not to obscure the message by talking about different causes at the same time. (For example, there is an obvious connection between the anti-war movement and the Central American issue, but when protests include both these questions as well as unemployment, women's rights, racial discrimination, and other injustices, the message is lost in a Babel.)

5. *Executive Accountability.* Congress is normally defensive on foreign policy matters, in part because these matters are outside the context of specific pieces of legislation. Nevertheless, the example of Vietnam shows that, armed with sufficient objective information, and without dealing with any specific legislation, Congress can change foreign policy simply by persistently focusing debate on the proper issues. Every effort should be made therefore, to provide Congress and others with the non-partisan policy studies and analyses of issues necessary for informed debate on our Central American policy. For instance, in regard to this policy, U.S. administrations have ignored or broken numerous laws. Among them are those dealing with:

a. Congressional powers to approve the waging of war in *whatever disguise.*

b. Congressional directives of the budgeting of economic and military aid and conditions on the use of such aid (i.e., human rights violations).

c. Congressional limits on funds for covert projects of the CIA and other intelligence agencies.

d. Congressional oversight of intelligence activities.

e. Congressional intent to limit or eliminate loans by multilateral lending agencies (i.e., the World Bank) to countries with a record of gross human rights violations.

Since World War II, the executive branch has increasingly encroached upon the powers of the legislature, thereby endangering the checks and balances established by the constitution. The Reagan administration is by no means the first to ignore Congress when waging war, but that does not make such actions less reprehensible.

Conclusion

The issues outlined for possible action involve difficult political decisions needing lengthy consultations and negotiations. In the meantime, it will be up to private groups to do the most they can to alleviate the suffering in Central America. Through networking in the United States and by providing people-to-people aid in Central America, they can prove to themselves—and to the rest of the world—that many Americans still uphold the principles for which their country stands. In this act of conscious protest against their government's policies, they can contribute to the growth of democratic structures in Central America and at the same time strengthen pluralism in the United States. If the seeds do not immediately bear fruit, that matters less than the sowing. Some eventually *will* grow and offer testament to the values and courage of those Americans who cared enough to dissent.

Footnotes

1. "Western Interests and U.S. Policy Options in the Caribbean Basin," the Atlantic Council, Dec. 12, 1983; "The Miami Report," University of Miami (Coral Gables, Fla.: n.d. [prepublication copy]); William M. LeoGrande, "The Not-So-Secret War in Central America," Special Report, Democratic Policy Committee, April 25, 1983; "Central America: Anatomy of a Conflict," edited by Robert Leiken of the Carnegie Endowment for Peace (Pergamon Press, 1984), as reported in *The Christian Science Monitor* (Jan. 24, 1984) and *In These Times*, (Jan. 18-24, 1984); "Changing Course: Blueprint for Peace in Central America and the Caribbean," Policy Alternatives for the Caribbean and Central America (PACCA) (Washington, D.C.: n.d. [galleys]).

2. In describing the different cultural contexts of the United States and Latin America, Eduardo Galeano, a well-known Uruguayan journalist, writes of a "structural censorship." "It means," he says, "that the ship cannot sail because there is no water in the sea. If only 5 per cent of the population of Latin America can buy a refrigerator, what percentage can buy books? What percentage can read them? Feel the need for them? Receive their influence?" (From THE WRITER AND HUMAN RIGHTS [Garden City, N.Y.: Anchor Press/Doubleday, 1983], p. 11.)

3. Donald E. Schulz, "El Salvador: Fear and Loathing in the Living Museum," *Revolution and Counterrevolution* (to be published by Westview), p. 335.

4. I.F. Stone, *In Time of Torment* (New York: Random House, 1968), pp. 173-74.

5. Interview, Tom Fox, editor, *National Catholic Reporter*, Feb., 1984.

6. "The Situation in Honduras," a Staff Report prepared for the Committee on Foreign Relations, U.S. Senate (Washington: 1982), p. 5; Phillip Berryman, *What's Wrong in Central America and What to Do about It* (Philadelphia: 1983), p. 30; "Changing Course...," Galley 6; *Latin America Weekly Report*, Dec. 16, 1983; Gary MacEoin, "Washington Undermines Fledgling Democracy," *The Witness*, Sept., 1983; The *New York Times*, Jan. 22, 1984.

7. "Central America," *Congressional Quarterly*, Dec. 31, 1983, pp. 2771-2780; Berryman, op. cit., pp. 9, 11; *Latin America Regional Reports Mexico & Central America*, Oct. 28, 1983; *The Guardian*, Oct. 19, 1983; "Changing Course...," op cit., Galleys 2 and 10; Robert Armstrong and Janet Shenk, *El Salvador The Face of Revolution* (Boston: South End Press, 1982), p. 30; *U.S. News & World Report*, Oct. 17, 1983.

8. Stephen Schlesinger and Stephen Kinzer, *Bitter Fruit* (Garden City, N.Y.: Doubleday, 1982).

9. In Brazil, where the Catholic Church has been active since the early 1960s in promoting grassroots participation through Christian base communities, the fruit of such work is just beginning to appear. In contrast, in Nicaragua, said the leader of a base community, the revolution, "happened so fast that there was no time to prepare the people." (Author's interviews in Sao Paulo, Brazil, Sept.-Oct., 1983, and Managua, Nicaragua, Jan., 1984.)

10. The *New York Times*, Aug. 21, 1983.

11. One expert, Robert Leiken, editor of the Carnegie Endowment for Peace study on Central America (see Note 1), calculates that two-thirds of the Salvadoran guerrilla forces belong to organizations that stress Salvadoran nationalism and non-alignment (as reported in *In These Times*, op. cit.). Writing on comparisons

between Vietnam and Central America, Roger Hillsman, State Department director of intelligence between 1961-63, said that during the Vietnam war dissidents in the Kennedy and Johnson administrations argued that "the insurgency was a nationalistic, anticolonialist movement" and that sending in foreign troops "would be self-defeating." "Foreign troops would recruit more peasants for the Viet Cong than they could possibly kill. As President Kennedy said, 'In the final analysis, it is their war'." (The *New York Times*, Aug. 21, 1983). See also Berryman, op. cit., p. 14.

12. For the statistics of poverty, see "Changing Course...," op. cit.; Berryman, op. cit.; Armstrong and Shenk, op. cit. Perhaps one of the most telling comparative statistics shows the difference between American and Central American consumers: on average the American housewife spends more on groceries in a month than a Central American family earns in a year.

13. Interviews with author, Jan. 22-28, 1984, Managua, Nicaragua. At the time of the author's visit no visa was required of U.S. citizens entering Nicaragua.

14. *Congressional Record*, July 15, 1983, p. S10101.

15. Schlesinger and Kinzer, op. cit.; Walter LaFeber, *Inevitable Revolutions* (New York: W.W. Norton, 1983); Penny Lernoux, *Cry of the People* (Penguin: 1982), pp. 81-202.

16. "Report of the National Bipartisan Commission on Central America" (Washington: Jan. 11, 1984).

17. Gallup Poll reports by George Gallup, March 31 and Aug. 21, 1983; AFP (Washington: Feb. 3, 1984); "Washington Focus," Washington Office on Latin America (Washington: Jan. 27, 1984).

18. For example, Art Pine, reporting from Honduras for *The Wall Street Journal*, described long bureaucratic delays in getting U.S. aid money through the pipeline for even the simplest projects, like school-desk designs. He also reported that "corruption keeps siphoning off materials and equipment," and noted that some projects are delayed by Honduras' inability to come up with the required one-quarter funding of any U.S.-supported project. (*The Wall Street Journal*, Feb. 7, 1984).

19. Lernoux, op. cit., pp. 81-202.

20. Luigi R. Einaudi and David F. Ronfeldt, *Internal Security and Military Assistance to Latin America in the 1970s: A First Statement* (Santa Monica, Calif.: RAND Corp., Dec. 1971), pp. 7-32.

21. Strauss quote from "Report of the National Bipartisan Commission on Central America," p. 131. Explained Viron Vaky, a former high-ranking State Department official: "What is at issue is not merely the amelioration of existing inequities and injustices, but the underlying power patterns which those inequities reflect. If the Salvadoran military, for example, decides to support a given reform measure, such as land reform, but remains the repository of political power, the underlying situation is not changed." (*In These Times* [Jan. 18-24, 1984], reporting on the Carnegie Endowment for Peace study on Central America (see Note 1).

22. In a piece in *Frontline* (Nov. 14, 1983), Victor Uno noted that "none of the farming cooperatives" that have survived the violence are solvent. Previous owners had sold off machinery and livestock, he said, and the peasants were unable to obtain financing for capitalization or to pay off the farms' previous debts. See also The *New York Times*, Dec. 15, 1983; *Envio Report*, Instituto Histórico Centroamericano

(Managua: Aug., 1983); *Congressional Quarterly,* op. cit.

23. Writing about El Salvador's land reform, Donald Schulz (see Note 3), points out that "the program had been accompanied by extensive corruption. Tens of millions of dollars had been poured into the Salvadoran Institute of Agrarian Transformation without any serious effort to audit the flow. (AID received information only through government meetings and written reports; no field work of its own was conducted because of security conditions.) The consequence, according to the Salvadoran Court of Accounts, was 'doubtful investments, exaggerated expenses, others improper, some laughable, and others not legally admissible from an accounting point of view'. Meanwhile, out in the field, many cooperatives were being forced to pay tribute to local military commanders, mostly in areas where there was no serious guerrilla threat." (p. 365.)

In a similar vein Adam Hochschild (The *New York Times,* Dec. 22, 1983) recalled how "a few years back the chief of staff of the Salvadoran Army was caught trying to sell $30 million worth of U.S. arms to two undercover U.S. police detectives posing as Mafiosi." After serving a sentence in the United States, he returned to El Salvador, where there has been no investigation.

Hochschild also tells of an army colonel and his associates who were found to have stolen more than $3.5 million in checks and money orders from El Salvador's post office last year. "The colonel denied everything and is believed to have fled to Miami."

Then there was Gen. Oswaldo Arellano, Honduras' strongman in the mid-1970s, who was forced to step down after the Securities and Exchange Commission revealed he and his sidekicks had taken $1.25 million in bribes from United Brands, the giant banana producer earlier known as United Fruit, or "el pulpo," the octopus. General Gustavo Alvarez, the current commander-in-chief and Reagan's man in Honduras, also did business with U.S. banana companies. As commander of a local battalion headquartered on Castle & Cooke's Honduran fiefdom, he was on the banana company's payroll. He repaid Castle by destroying a local cooperative the Americans objected to, because the workers wanted to market their bananas independently of Castle at better prices. (Lernoux, op. cit., pp. 115-19; MacEoin, op. cit.)

24. *Maclean's,* Nov. 28, 1983; "Epilogue: The Report of the Kissinger Commission," PACCA (n.d.); *National Catholic Reporter,* Jan. 27, 1984; Schulz, op. cit., pp. 409-10; *Newsweek,* Dec. 5, 1983; *Latin America Regional Reports Mexico & Central America,* Oct. 28, 1983; Lydia Chavez, "El Salvador," The *New York Times Magazine,* Dec. 11, 1983; *Latin America Weekly Report,* Dec. 2, 1983.

25. "Public Opinion on Central America," Special Report No. 61, Democratic Policy Committee (Washington: Aug. 4, 1983); Ross K. Baker, "The Bipartisan Trap," *Worldview,* Aug., 1983.

26. Tad Szulc, in "El Salvador Is Spanish for Vietnam" (*Penthouse,* Sept., 1983), points out that "to carry out a landing on the long Salvadoran beaches with no significant port facilities, U.S. Marines or Army troops would have to be shipped all the way from California, a complex enterprise. Once landed, they would have to fight through inhospitable terrain inhabited by a presumably hostile population–nationalism would certainly rally even pro-regime Salvadorans against a U.S. invasion–to reach San Salvador, the capital. Then, as in Vietnam, the question would arise how to beat the guerrillas on their own turf, an effort doubtlessly

requiring an actual occupation of much of El Salvador. And even an occupation would not necessarily mean victory."

27. *Le Monde Diplomatique en Español,* Nov., 1983.

28. *Latin America Weekly Report,* Sept. 16, 1983.

29. "National Campaign for Peace in Central America" (Washington: n.d.); *The Wall Street Journal,* Jan. 12, 1984.

30. Berryman, op, cit., p. 21, citing "Carta de los Mandos Medios del Ejército acerca del Diálogo," *El Día* (Mexico City), Nov. 6, 1982.

31. Tom Fox, op. cit.

32. *Latin America Weekly Report,* Sept. 23, 1983; *The Nation,* Dec. 24, 1983; AFP (San Salvador: Feb. 9, 1984); Berryman, op. cit., pp. 41-42; Schulz, op. cit., p. 362.

33. Anonymous, "Dissent Paper on El Salvador and Central America," Nov., 1980.

34. "National Campaign...," op. cit.; UPI (San Salvador: Dec. 25, 1983); "El Salvador: America's War without Honor," Commission on United States-Central American Relations (Washington: n.d.); Berryman, op. cit., p. 18; "Changing Course...," op. cit., Galley 23.

35. Berryman, op. cit., pp. 19-25; Schlesinger and Kinzer, op. cit., pp. 227-55; LaFeber, op. cit., pp. 164-71.

36. Schulz, op. cit., pp. 826-27.

37. Interviews with Nicaraguan officials, Managua, Jan., 1984; Schulz, op. cit., p. 829.

38. Jim Chapin and Jack Clark, in an article for *Commonweal* (Jan. 3, 1983), debunk the Carter and Reagan administration theory that a political center can be found on the extreme right: "You can't conduct a social revolution under the aegis of the class which opposes the revolution. It would be as if the British were to have supported the South in the American Civil War as a means of gaining the abolition of American slavery." See also Berryman, op. cit., pp. 10, 12, 51; Schulz, op. cit., p. 382.

39. Said a Venezuelan foreign ministry official of the peace process: "There will be no peace without democracy, and democracy means compromise, and compromise means accepting the right of each country to decide how it will carry on its own affairs. We have to realize that this is a long process and that there are no shortcuts." *(Latin America Regional Reports Mexico & Central America,* Oct. 28, 1983).

40. Among Contadora's principal proposals are:
    a. an inventory of military installations, arms, and soldiers by each of the Central American nations to establish an arms control and reduction policy.
    b. a census by country of all military advisers or foreigners who could serve in that capacity and a deadline for their reduction and departure.
    c. banishment of armed groups which use the territory of one country for hostile acts against another.
    d. an effort to discover the areas, routes, and means used for the illegal interzonal and foreign arms traffic in order to stop it.
    e. establishment of communications mechanisms to prevent and resolve incidents between states.
    f. promotion of national reconciliation based on justice, freedom, and democracy and the means to encourage dialogue among countries.
    g. full guarantee of human rights and fulfillment of constitutional and interna-

tional treaty obligations to such guarantees.

　　h. enactment or revision of electoral legislation for elections guaranteeing effective popular participation.

　　i. the institution or revision of norms guaranteeing the existence and participation of diverse political parties.

　　j. adoption of an electoral calendar and measures to guarantee the participation of all parties under equal conditions.

　　k. an increase in refugee aid programs and the establishment of the means for voluntary repatriation, through the cooperation of governments in coordination with national and international humanitarian organizations.

　　l. negotiations to obtain external resources to revitalize the Central American economies.

　　m. development of regional trade and improved access to international markets for Central American products.

　　n. the establishment of just economic and social structures which consolidate an authentically democratic system and allow free access by the people to employment, education, health, and culture. (Source: AP [Panama City, Jan. 9, 1984].)

　　As observed by the Kissinger Commission, the pace of Contadora negotiations will depend on the United States' response. (See "Report...," op. cit., p. 120.)

41. *Latin America Weekly Report*, Aug. 5, Oct. 21, and Nov. 18, 1983; *Covert Action*, No. 18, Winter, 1983; *Congressional Record*, July 20, 1983, p. E3606; Christopher Hitchens, "Minority Report," *The Nation*, Oct. 8, 1983; *First Principles*, Vol. 8, No. 5, May/June, 1983; LeoGrande, op. cit.; *Newsweek*, Aug. 1, 1983; "Concerning U.S. Military and Paramilitary Operations in Nicaragua," Markup before the Committee on Foreign Affairs, House of Representatives (Washington: U.S. Government Printing Office, May 18, June 6 and 7, 1983).

42. Berryman, op. cit., p. 26-27, 49; *Covert Action*, No. 20, Winter, 1984.

43. Nicaraguan government sources calculate that losses from attacks by the CIA's *contras* have cost the country $453 million since mid-1982. U.S. veto of loans to Nicaragua in such multilateral institutions as the Inter-American Development Bank has cost Nicaragua another $112.5 million; Nicaragua also lost its U.S. sugar market after Washington cut its quota by 90 percent *(Latin America Regional Reports Mexico & Central America*, Jan. 13, 1984; *Journal of Commerce*, Aug. 5, 1983).

　　Contrary to Washington's claims that the *contras'* activities have helped pressure the Sandinista government to open up the political process, quite the opposite has happened. For example, last January, when the government was gearing up for the campaign leading to 1985 elections, armed attacks on Nicaragua's northern borders persuaded the Sandinistas to "postpone the process indefinitely." They later reversed the decision, but as Sergio Ramirez, a novelist and non-military member of the three-man junta, said, the best guarantee for elections is to leave the Nicaraguans alone (author's interviews, Managua, Jan., 1984; *In These Times*, Sept. 21, 1983).

44. *Congressional Record*, July 15, 1983, op. cit.

45. *South*, July 9, 1983.

46. Author's interviews, Managua, Jan., 1984.

47. Most Nicaraguans belong to a community organization. The majority follow—or at least do not think to question—the political orientation of the Sandinista leader-

48. Latin American leftists are keenly aware of the fate of Salvador Allende's experiment with socialism in Chile, and in Central America the memory of the CIA's intervention in Guatemala against a reformist government is still vivid. The threat of destabilization or armed intervention only contributes to the siege mentality of the Sandinista leadership, whereas a political approach reduces tensions and contributes to an opening of the democratic process.

49. From both a macro- and micro-economic viewpoint, it makes sense to link agriculture to other sectors of the economy, such as construction and industry, which normally feed on the foreign exchange from agricultural exports without contributing significantly to employment or overall economic growth. All the Central American countries depend on a few traditional exports (i.e., coffee, cotton, sugar, bananas), in most cases because of mismanagement. (Where, is the logic, for instance, in spending hundreds of millions of dollars on food imports which these countries could grow themselves? They fail to do so because most of the land is used for exports like coffee and sugar. The large landowners' claim that exports pay for imports does not hold up on economic or social grounds, since the only people to benefit from such a system are themselves.)

As shown in Nicaragua, agrarian reform, or the redistribution of inefficiently cultivated land, is the first step toward the production of badly needed grains, ship on national matters, but there is a surprising amount of counterdirection from the local groups to the junta when decisions affect community life. Last year, for instance, the government prepared a radical urban reform decree that would have given every person renting a house instant ownership. As one informed South American observer noted, the "notion that all people should have the right to their own home was completely romantic and unrealistic." When the government sent the reform to the council of state (a quasi-parliament) for rubberstamping, there was unexpected opposition; by the time it reached the community level the uproar was near unanimous: it turned out that quite a few poor people depended on the rent from a hut to make ends meet. The government dropped the reform.

A similar give-and-take process can be observed at the government's weekly "Face the People" meetings with neighborhood groups. On issues affecting their daily lives, the people are critical and demand solutions without fear of reprisal. Government officials explain why certain things happen—for example, why it is necessary to tear down two houses to make way for a road in the area—take note of the criticisms and, by most accounts, try to act on them.

The extent to which such informal democracy is institutionalized, say thoughtful Nicaraguans, depends on the growth of community groups. While unions and block committees are elected democratically, the directors of such mass organizations as women's and youth groups are still appointed by the government. On the other hand, community groups so not seem to perceive a need to elect such people, since they are more preoccupied with local concerns like the repair of a school bus or the replacement of a tractor.

Consequently, informed Nicaraguans, including some government officials, say that at this point on the unknown path it is too early to judge the likelihood of a broad-based political society or a top-down Marxist model. What is not in doubt is the revolution's popularity: the government has only to call for volunteers to pick coffee or serve in the militia fighting the *contras* for thousands to immediately enlist. (Author's interviews, Managua, Jan., 1984.)

half of which Central America imports. Peasant production of grains (usually in cooperatives) shows "a tendency to invest [the surplus] in livestock, permanent plantations, and farm infrastructure"–or to break the pattern of a single crop. Increased grain production in turn feeds livestock, dairy, and poultry production to meet rising local demands for meat and dairy products. The aim of such diversified production, at least in Nicaragua, is to satisfy local food needs and export earning requirments, while also integrating rural and urban areas through agroindustrial projects (i.e., sugar and livestock processing) and the construction of needed infrastructure like roads, storage facilities, and markets. ("An Alternative Policy for Central America and the Caribbean," Summary and Conclusions of Policy Workshop held in The Hague, June 6-25, 1983 [Institute of Social Studies: The Hague, 1983], pp. 39-47.)

50. Author's interviews, Managua, Jan., 1984.

51. One communications expert, David H. Rothman, has suggested an "Electronic Peace Corps" for the Third World, using satellite links and relatively inexpensive computers for educational and information exchanges for people in government, private industry and social services (*Federal Times*, Jan. 23, 1984). Some Latin American countries already are discussing the use of networks of cheap computers to teach students unable to obtain a place in the overcrowded university system.

52. Author's interviews, Managua, Jan., 1984.

53. "Report...," op. cit., p. 130.

54. Most of the Central American countries have been forced to seek a rescheduling of their debt; some, such as Costa Rica and Honduras, have repeatedly fallen behind on interest repayment. The austerity squeeze has contributed to a sharp increase in unemployment and a downturn in industrial production at the same time that commodity prices have remained weak. Last year most of the area registered zero economic growth. Central American sources claim the region needs $23 billion in new capital just to regain the 1980 standard of living (*Latin America Regional Reports Mexico & Central America*, Oct. 28, 1983).

55. Contrary to the Reagan administration's claim that a "brown tide" of "feet people" will inundate the United States if a left-wing government comes to power in El Salvador, most of the people who have fled Central America in the past four years are poor peasants who have been starved and terrorized from their land by right-wing regimes. Patricia Weiss Fagen of the Washington-based Refugee Policy Center points out that under Somoza nearly one million Nicaraguans fled their country, whereas most returned after Somoza's downfall.

56. As admitted by Elliott Abrams, assistant secretary of state for human rights, "The battle for Central America is a battle for the high moral ground. And it is much harder for us to win that battle when a lot of church groups are opposing us and saying we don't have it." (*The Wall Street Journal*, Dec. 8, 1983.)

Penny Lernoux is an investigative reporter with more than two decades of experience in Latin America. Her book, CRY OF THE PEOPLE (1980) documented the clash between the changing Catholic Church and U.S. corporate interests. It received widespread acclaim, including Columbia University's Maria Moors Cabot Award and the Sidney Hillman Foundation Book Award.

Born in Los Angeles, Ms. Lernoux is a Phi Beta Kappa graduate of the University of Southern California, where she began her writing career as city editor of the *Daily Trojan*. She first went to Latin America with the U.S. Information Agency in Bogotá and Rio de Janeiro. In 1964 she joined the California-based Copley News Service, and for a decade reported from Caracas, Buenos Aires and Bogotá. Since 1975, she has worked as a freelance writer for numerous U.S. publications, including Harper's, Atlantic, Newsweek and The Nation, for which she is the Latin American correspondent.

During her years in Latin America, Ms. Lernoux has travelled from the Rio Grande to Tierra del Fuego covering coups and revolutions, and interviewing many of the region's leaders, including presidents, generals, businessmen, labor leaders and Church figures. On occasion she has had to wear a disguise in order to cover a story. In a Bolivian tin mine where miners believe priests and women bring bad luck, they threw dynamite at Ms. Lernoux. During the Somoza regime in Nicaragua, she visited the northeastern rain forests disguised as a nun in order to document reports of peasant massacres by Somoza's National Guard.

To protect her sources from police informers, she has conducted interviews in such places as the middle of a forest or travelling from place to place in a moving car. In one case, she spent 50 hours on a bus travelling through the Brazilian Amazon in order to interview the occupants, including several Bishops persecuted by the Brazilian military regime. Before departure, anonymous callers threatened to blow up the bus.

Ms. Lernoux has received two citations from the Overseas Press Club of America, the Tom Wallace Inter-American Press Association Award, Sigma Delta Chi's magazine award and an honorary Ph.D. in Letters from Kenyon College as well as grants from the Alicia Patterson Foundation and the Fund for Investigative Journalism. In 1983 she held the Hubert Humphrey Visiting Professor's Chair at Macalester College in Minnesota where she taught courses on Latin America and international banking.

Ms. Lernoux lives in Bogotá, Colombia. She is married and has one daughter.

****

IN BANKS WE TRUST by Penny Lernoux was published by Anchor Press/Doubleday on February 24, 1984.

****